API Security

Salt Security Special Edition

by Michael Isbitski

for **dummies**®

A Wiley Brand

API Security For Dummies®, Salt Security Special Edition

Published by
John Wiley & Sons, Inc.
111 River St.
Hoboken, NJ 07030-5774
www.wiley.com

ISBN 978-1-119-85476-0 (pbk); ISBN 978-1-119-85477-7 (ebk)

Publisher's Acknowledgments

For general information on our other products and services, or how to create a custom *For Dummies* book for your business or organization, please contact our Business Development Department in the U.S. at 877-409-4177, contact info@dummies.biz, or visit www.wiley.com/go/custompub. Some of the people who helped bring this book to market include the following:

Project Manager: Chad R. Sievers

Acquisitions Editor: Ashley Coffey

Editorial Manager: Rev Mengle

Business Development Representative: Matt Cox

Project Editor: Vivek Lakshmikanth

SKY10040023_121622

Table of Contents

Introduction

Application programming interfaces (APIs) serve as the building blocks of modern application architecture and system design. They create the on-ramps to the digital world, keep everyone connected, facilitate business, make digital transformation possible, and continuously evolve modern computing. In all your digital activities — across employee business applications, ecommerce sites, health services, connected cars, banking applications, home automation, and mobile apps — you're using APIs. The fact that APIs enable so much sharing of data and services makes them prime targets for attackers. Security practitioners must adapt for the world of APIs so they're better equipped to secure their organization's applications and data.

About This Book

API Security For Dummies, Salt Security Custom Edition, describes how application architecture has evolved, how APIs are the foundation of modern design, how those API foundations are threatened, and how the API building blocks can be secured. This book is conveniently organized into five chapters that do the following:

>> Arrive at a working definition of modern APIs so you can dig into the many facets of API security.

>> Describe how application architecture has evolved, how cloud technologies have impacted designs, and how DevOps practices accelerate API growth.

>> Detail API implementation and operational activities that factor into security, including documentation, testing, mediation, and integration.

>> Describe how attackers abuse the business logic of APIs and automate attacks to increase likelihood of success or do further damage.

>> Increase awareness around the OWASP API Security Top 10 and the common API security gaps it spotlights.

>> Highlight the technological capabilities you need to secure APIs throughout their life cycles, including discovery, protection, and remediation.

>> Present ten prioritized things you can do now to start securing APIs for your organization.

Foolish Assumptions

Although this book is written primarily for technical readers with some level of experience in modern computing, everyone can benefit from the information. I make very few assumptions when writing about the world of APIs and API security. I assume you've browsed a website or used mobile application in recent years and are inclined to dig deeper into some inner workings. Knowing how your digital world functions and is built on the foundations of APIs is interesting in its own right. And it's also enlightening as to how the digital world can be threatened by malicious actors.

Icons Used in This Book

Throughout this book, I use icons to call attention to important information. Here's what you can expect:

TIP

This icon indicates that the information is useful and can save time for a given activity.

REMEMBER

When you see this icon, make sure you read and understand the surrounding text. The tidbit points out important information that's worth reiterating.

WARNING

This icon alerts you to a potential issue or pitfall. I point out where others have made mistakes in the hopes that it saves you time and spares some heartburn.

Beyond the Book

I can cover only so much in this short book, particularly with a complex topic. If you find yourself hungry for more knowledge on API security, just go to www.salt.security.

Chapter **1**

Understanding APIs

I f you're looking for a primer and background on APIs, you've landed on the right chapter. Here I arrive at a working definition of application programming interface (API), particularly as it relates to the Internet and web design. I cover some resulting impacts of APIs to modern application and cloud-native design.

Defining APIs

Understanding API consumer types and API protocols is key to selecting the most effective security techniques and controls available to you. *Application programming interfaces (APIs)* are sometimes used as a synonym for functions or libraries referenced regularly in code. For example, web APIs are a specific type of API designed for use in web designs and communications. Web API design patterns have existed for more than 20 years, emerging from service-oriented architecture (SOA) and back-end services powering applications via web protocols. The following sections discuss in greater detail the types of APIs and how APIs work.

Recognizing the common types of APIs

The term *consumption* refers to the API caller making a request to an API to exercise functionality, query data, or manipulate data.

The range of API types has evolved substantially over the years to account for different business cases and usage models. Some of the common API types include the following:

>> **External APIs:** These APIs support mobilized workforces and customers accessing services from anywhere. As the name implies, they're exposed to users outside a protected network or the Internet, often with relaxed network restrictions. Authentication and authorization may or may not be used.

>> **Public APIs:** Public APIs are a type of external API designed for consumption by users and machines across the Internet. They have relaxed access controls or are designed for anonymous access to increase consumption.

>> **Open APIs:** These APIs appear more frequently with open banking initiatives including the financial industry. They help promote innovation in a given industry, improve levels of service integration, and provide freedom for customers to transact or access data anywhere. Authentication and delegated authorization are usually in place.

>> **Internal APIs:** These APIs are usually deployed and operated within a restricted network environment of a data center or private cloud segment. They're designed to be consumed by other applications or users in that restricted network. Authentication and authorization may be in place but may be relaxed because exposure is limited.

>> **Partner APIs:** Organizations sometimes provide limited access to internal APIs to select external suppliers to power and expand their digital supply chains. The extent of access control lies somewhere between that of internal and external APIs.

>> **Third-party APIs:** These APIs, often consumed as cloud-delivered services, or software as a service (SaaS), help organizations move faster without re-creating functionality or incurring more technical debt.

>> **Acquired APIs:** These APIs are less of a design choice and more of a type of inheritance. Organizations inherit these APIs as a type of dependency as they acquire, integrate, and deploy commercial and open-source software packages.

Identifying API protocols

API protocols impact choices around architecture, testing tools, and runtime security controls. Protocols are also sometimes intertwined with API schema definitions, which you must account for as part of API documentation. Chapter 2 covers API documentation and schema.

For now, think of the *API protocol* as the means for how you communicate with an API, whereas the *API schema* defines what data should look like in those communications or what functionality is available.

Here are some of the most common API protocols you're likely to see:

>> **Representational state transfer (REST):** RESTful design helps enable client-server architecture patterns and separation of the interface from back-end services. One of the trickier concepts with REST is that API endpoints can look drastically different from one organization to the next depending how they're designed and coded. Elements of a URL structure may represent functions or variables. HTTP methods may also be used differently than expected.

>> **GraphQL:** GraphQL is a query language, but it can also be used to manipulate data. Facebook created GraphQL to deal with two problems. The first was to reduce excessive web API calls. The second was to deal with fetching too much or too little data that is sometimes inherent with REST API design. The benefits to front-end performance are generating more interest in GraphQL, though REST APIs will still likely remain in the picture.

>> **Remote procedure call (RPC)-based protocols:** You may still see the terms JavaScript object notation (JSON)-RPC and extensible Markup Language (XML)-RPC, where JSON and XML denote the encoding format used in API requests. Google created *gRPC remote procedure call (gRPC)*, which has gained in popularity for speedy microservice communication. Unlike REST and GraphQL though, you rarely see gRPC as the protocol of choice for browser-based front ends.

>> **Simple object access protocol (SOAP):** SOAP APIs are still seen in some internal APIs and business applications. However, SOAP API implementations are often viewed as too heavyweight and have largely been supplanted by REST API design.

Designing Modern Applications with APIs

APIs have significantly changed the way that development teams create applications. Whether your organization is building, acquiring, or integrating APIs, the impacts to front-end design, business functionality, and data exchange are significant. APIs are also prominent within microservices architecture (MSA) and cloud-native design patterns. Continue reading the following sections for more details.

Decoupling front ends and back ends

When most users and even practitioners think of an application, they're thinking of a *front-end interface* or graphical user interface (GUI). In most application designs, front-end interfaces are decoupled from back-end services and APIs so that any individual component can be updated iteratively and more easily. Front-end code can be script running in a web browser, or it may be native mobile code such as a mobile app designed for Android and iOS.

Organizations often attempt to secure and harden the front-end code that is installed on user devices, but this proposition can be difficult given what's in the realm of control of the organization. For mobilized employee apps, this approach may still be technically feasible for bring your own device (BYOD) and corporate-owned, personally enabled (COPE) scenarios. However, for mobile apps destined for customers, patients, or citizens, an organization has little control over end-user devices where client-side code protections are often circumvented.

Considering impacts from microservices architecture

In some cases, the terms *microservices* and *APIs* are used interchangeably. However, to help you better understand, keep in mind the following words and definitions:

>> **Microservice:** It's a service designed to do one thing and one thing only. This design pattern contrasts with monolithic design where a system or service is designed to do many things. The idea is that a microservice brings easier-to-understand code and looser coupling between services.

>> **Microservices architecture (MSA):** It's an architecture pattern where a system is composed of many interoperating microservices. An MSA provides benefits like improved design flexibility, improved continuous delivery, and faster service and infrastructure startup.

>> **Monoliths:** *Monoliths* are designed to do many things, which consequently can make them difficult to upgrade or maintain. They remain in existence despite how they may seem taboo and how industry focus has shifted to MSA. They may be an organization's preferred design pattern based on pedigree or developer experience.

REMEMBER

A microservice's functionality doesn't need to be exposed outside of the microservice environment. If your organization wants to expose microservice functionality, then an API is the way to do it. Inner microservice communications may use a protocol such as gRPC, whereas functionality may be exposed to users that are external to the microservice environment via REST or GraphQL APIs. It's not uncommon for APIs to be mediated by API gateways. Chapter 2 touches more on the topic of API mediation.

MSA brings increased operational complexity because of the high number of distributed services that you must deploy and orchestrate. Organizations usually have a mixture of both monoliths and microservices. In practice, many architectures resemble something in between.

Altering the API picture: Cloud-native's role

Cloud-native has a few meanings depending what IT circle you sit in. The broadest definition is that a design or architecture exhibits cloud traits and makes use of technologies that power cloud service providers. Common cloud traits include web scale capacity and elasticity, where the compute you need to run an application or service is almost infinite, bound only by the available hardware in a cloud provider's data centers that is largely abstracted from you.

The following technologies enable cloud computing:

>> **Virtualization:** *Virtualization* is a way to abstract hardware from the operating system using a hypervisor. You can run many virtual machines on a given physical host, often described in terms of density. By packing more virtual machines on a given host, you can make better use of the hardware and ensure it doesn't sit idle. Virtual machines are used readily to power applications and services, but virtual machines must be lightweight and highly performant if they're to service MSAs.

>> **Containerization:** *Containerization* involves packaging applications and their dependencies into containers to further increase density by abstracting the operating system from applications and services. Containers improve portability and environment consistency. Containers are often used as the unit of compute to power microservices within MSA.

Cloud-native maps to the world of APIs in a few ways, but the two most common are as follows:

>> Organizations pair containerization and virtualization to limit the blast radius in the event of compromised API code, container runtimes, or hypervisors.

>> Entire infrastructures can be declared and operated via APIs, for example, with container platforms like Kubernetes and cloud service providers.

IN THIS CHAPTER

» Identifying problems with API
documentation and analysis

» Understanding API security testing
methods

» Mediating APIs to improve observability
and enforce policies

Chapter **2**
Laying the Foundations for API Security

Traditional approaches to securing APIs are numerous, including testing and mediation. This chapter examines these approaches in greater detail.

Documenting APIs

API documentation serves a range of security and nonsecurity purposes throughout the API life cycle. Documentation gives your organization a couple of primary advantages:

» It provides details on how to communicate with APIs, the functionality they provide, and the data they exchange so you can better understand your API attack surface.

» It serves as input into other activities including design reviews, security testing, operations, and protection.

WARNING

Like all forms of documentation, teams inevitably neglect to document APIs or new functionality as they iterate. This reality leads to a type of *environment drift*, also referred to as *API drift*, that leaves massive gaps in your API inventory and security posture.

TIP

Document APIs that you build and use that data to feed an API inventory or catalog. Include third-party APIs where adequate documentation is provided by the supplier. Mitigate gaps in your API inventory by continuously scanning environments and analyzing traffic to discover new API endpoints and functions.

The following sections touch on a couple more points your organization needs to remember as it documents its APIs.

Steering clear of traditional documentation approaches

Avoid approaching API documentation as a traditional documentation exercise with the goal of producing lengthy text documents or visual diagrams as artifacts. Written documents, slides, or visual diagrams are sometimes required for compliance or as part of design reviews.

Some organizations tend to carry over security from traditional compliance and waterfall approaches. However, many IT organizations start to feel increased pressure as development teams adopt agile methodologies and DevOps practices that often come as part of a package deal with API development.

Traditional documentation can be useful for secure design reviews and threat modeling. However, traditional forms of documentation are notoriously difficult to generate and maintain. API drift can be worse in these cases, and API documentation likely won't reflect the reality of your production deployment even with extra manpower allocated to documenting all changes.

Working with API schema definitions

The API schema definition formats are designed to make your life easier. Schema can be defined and documented during API creation. The schema definitions are also reusable for testing, integration, publishing, and operations. Many design, mocking, and development tools can autogenerate API schema definitions as you integrate or code an API.

You can use these features to reduce documentation workload and avoid headaches later. Open-source software packages that include web APIs also commonly include the relevant API schema definitions in the corresponding code repository (such as git) or package manager (such as npm) you obtain them from.

Most commonly for REST APIs, these machine formats include Swagger or OpenAPI specification (OAS). Depending on your API design, development, or publishing tooling, other formats like RAML or API Blueprint may be present. And if you're exploring GraphQL APIs, then also expect to work with GraphQL schema definitions.

Testing APIs

A specific focus within shift-left API security practices is *securing the build pipeline,* which requires that teams get security tooling plugged into continuous integration/continuous delivery (CI/CD) build pipelines and git-based developer workflows. Securing build pipelines requires a range of security-testing tools including dependency analyzers, static analyzers, dynamic analyzers, schema validators, fuzzers, and vulnerability scanners. The type of security tooling that is needed varies based on what artifacts are moving through the pipeline, what must be built, and where must it be delivered.

The following sections examine the advantages and disadvantages of security testing within build pipelines.

Utilizing application security testing tools

Static application security testing (SAST) can be used to analyze original source code for potential weaknesses and vulnerabilities. It's often run when code is committed to version control or during build stages. Meanwhile, *dynamic application security testing (DAST)* can be used to analyze a running application for exploitable conditions. It's often initiated prior to production delivery or used in production continuously because the application must be running on infrastructure.

WARNING

SAST and DAST can uncover weaknesses and exploitable conditions in your custom API code. However, these scanning methods can't uncover business logic flaws that attackers target and abuse. Business logic — and how you design and code APIs — is unique to your organization. As a result, the code that represents your business logic rarely follows well-defined patterns where SAST or DAST signatures can be built accordingly.

Most tools don't go deep in testing authentication or authorization beyond cursory checks such as detecting weak forms of authentication like basic and digest access, or the testing tool may only analyze how credentials are input, passed, or stored. Some DAST tools can check for privilege escalation weaknesses, but doing so requires multiple runs of the tool against a given app and its API. Unfortunately, many organizations push tight release windows and time is at a premium.

DAST tools are notorious for running for extended periods of time for complex applications. Budget time accordingly for build pipeline scans to complete or make scans nonblocking so as not to hold up releases.

SAST and DAST have always had their shortcomings. The problem is worsened in the world of APIs. Yes, you should run them against your custom application and API code, but acknowledge that these scanners aren't designed to detect all types of issues. The importance of behavior analysis in runtime for APIs can't be stressed enough (refer to Chapter 4 for more details).

Using API schema validators

A form of static analysis, API schema validators are often pitched as the DevOps-friendly solution for build pipeline security. The pitch often goes like this: "Give us your schema definitions; we can scan your APIs, make sure they're conformant, and check for vulnerabilities."

However, you should be aware of a few issues that exist with the schema validation approach:

>> **Not everything needs to be defined in API schema.** API specification formats like OAS and Swagger don't require that you define all fields or functions in the API documentation. Developers commonly forget to document something fully, particularly if they aren't working within API design tools like Postman.

>> **Many organizations are lackluster at documenting.** Humans are notoriously bad at documenting and especially documenting everything fully. A lack of documentation isn't a problem specific to developers. OAS can help in that it's self-documenting, but it still requires manual effort. Some tooling may also be better at generating the OAS definition than others.

>> **API drift happens as a matter of course.** Deviations from the original specification and what is running in production are common. API drift parallels one of the biggest problems that organizations run into with secure design review and threat modeling processes. Sometimes what you intend to build ends up looking much different than the real-world product.

REMEMBER

Any AST or schema analysis tooling you select should be integrated and automated to serve the pipeline. Tools should work within established git workflow and CI/CD processes. Scanning manually, finding issues, and spitting out a report aren't enough. Such an approach won't work for agile methodologies or DevOps practices that most organizations are embracing.

Schema validation and enforcement is the old paradigm of positive security in new clothes. Instead of security teams having to create rules or signatures, the burden is shifted to development teams. Schema validation can only identify some exploitable conditions and misconfigurations. Schema analysis can't identify business logic flaws.

Mediating 101: APIs and the Relevant Mechanisms

Although it's possible to directly expose an API via a web or application server, this practice is less common in typical enterprise architectures. API mediation can be achieved through several other mechanisms including network load balancers, application delivery controllers, Kubernetes ingress controllers, sidecar proxies, and service mesh ingresses.

Understanding that you can mediate and observe API traffic at multiple points in an enterprise architecture is what you need to know here. Having a basic idea of the various mediation points is critical to API security so you're seeing all traffic, are able to enforce as appropriate, and remediate quickly. The actual selection of a particular mediation mechanism or the point in an architecture where you'd elect to proxy API traffic is beyond the scope of this book.

These sections examine in plain English what you need to know about mediation and APIs.

Deploying proxies — reverse and forward

Design patterns like API facade and front end for back ends involve putting a proxying mediation layer in front of APIs. API mediation is commonly achieved by deploying proxies of one (or both) of the following types:

>> **Reverse proxy:** A *reverse proxy* analyzes and acts on traffic that is inbound to an API or service. For example, you may want to proxy inbound calls to monitor API usage or consumption.

>> **Forward proxy:** A *forward proxy* analyzes and acts on traffic that is outbound from an API or service. For example, you may want to proxy outbound calls to an API dependency that is delivered as a cloud-hosted software-as-a-service (SaaS).

REMEMBER

Business drivers and use cases will drive adoption of both proxy deployment types. Mediation provides a wide range of benefits including improved visibility, accelerated delivery, increased operational flexibility, and improved enforcement capabilities, particularly when it comes to API access control. Expect to see both forward and reverse proxies in any given architecture. Proxies are an area of API practice that quickly get into the realm of infrastructure and operations, network engineering, and enterprise architecture rather than application development.

Functioning as API mediation points

In most enterprise architectures, you'll find a mix of proxying mechanisms that mediate API requests and responses:

>> **Network load balancers (NLB):** *Network load balancers (NLB)* may be physical hardware or software-defined, and

they're responsible for routing requests dynamically between servers and services to balance network load.

» **Application delivery controllers (ADC):** *Application delivery controllers (ADC)* are like their NLB counterparts, though they typically include more functionality focused on application-specific routing, load-balancing, and caching. In some cases, ADC and NLB are interchangeable and can just be a matter of vendor language.

» **API gateways:** *API gateways* are designed specifically for mediating API traffic. They can also help with message translation and bridging between different protocols for inner and outer architecture.

» **API management (APIM):** *API management (APIM)* suites provide full life cycle capabilities on top of API gateways alone. They typically enable an organization to unify policies across gateways and API endpoints, provide rolled-up monitoring, and enable developer or partner self-service. APIM still relies on API gateways as a mediating proxy mechanism to enable their functionality and enforce policies.

REMEMBER

If an organization is rapidly embracing MSA, more than likely the organization has ingress controllers for Kubernetes and service meshes. Such ingresses are a mashup of API gateways and NLBs, and they may support multiple protocols depending on the design of the microservices. Proxies may also be deployed more local to a given workload that powers a microservice or API. Such proxies are typically referred to as *sidecar proxies*. Sidecar proxies function as a type of loopback proxy, where all traffic flowing into or out of a workload must go through the sidecar proxy.

Enforcing policy with API management

APIM offerings usually provide a set of capabilities to satisfy some use cases. Those capabilities commonly include the following:

» **Network security:** Like NLBs or ADCs, network connectivity can be restricted to APIs in an API gateway. Commonly this includes IP address allow and deny lists to restrict which origin IP addresses can communicate to a given API, rate limits to restrict how frequently requests can be made, and transport encryption with TLS to provide confidentiality and integrity of messages in transit.

>> **Authentication and authorization:** Organizations often enforce access control at API gateways so that API calls are authenticated and authorized. Common protocols include OIDC for authentication and OAuth2 for authorization. Token translation is usually offered as well, such as where an API implementation requires integration with older protocols like security assertion markup language (SAML).

>> **Basic threat protection:** By design, the mediation mechanisms already offer message filtering and protocol translation. Many APIM offerings provide basic rules to block malicious character sets commonly used in injection attacks. The other threat protection capability includes restricting incoming API requests based on API schema definitions or manual configuration. Restrictions can be placed on parameter lengths, parameter values, array sizes, and more.

WARNING

Enable APIM security controls when possible if doing so doesn't break API integrations with other systems. These settings can mitigate some types of API attacks, but they won't protect you from most forms of API abuse and business logic attacks.

IN THIS CHAPTER

» Differentiating between API attacks
and application attacks

» Looking at the OWASP API Security
Top 10

» Identifying patterns of automated
attacks

Chapter 3

Getting the Lowdown on API Attacks

This chapter clarifies in plain English how API attacks differ from application attacks. You also can read more about the OWASP API Security Top 10, which is a good starting point for understanding common API flaws. This chapter also covers automated attack patterns like brute forcing, credential stuffing, and scraping that almost always target APIs specifically.

Understanding How API Attacks Differ from Application Attacks

API attack patterns vary from what practitioners are used to within the network security and application security domains. Attacks may borrow from both domains, or more commonly, they're unique to API use cases and business logic specifically.

Attackers exploit misconfigurations in infrastructure controls, vulnerabilities in code, or some combination of the two. Leaving security to a development team was already a poor strategy, and some shift-left approaches and misguided DevOps practices have pushed responsibility too heavily onto development teams.

Developers may lack expertise in infrastructure and security concepts, which inevitably results in gaps in API security.

Attackers use your front-end applications to connect to your back-end APIs and to help decipher your business logic. Attackers also relish the fact that modern applications are highly interconnected with many first-party and third-party APIs, any one of which might be exploitable.

The front-end application is only a means to an end

Security teams sometimes attempt to secure APIs by protecting endpoints or hardening client applications. For some API consumption scenarios, you simply can't secure the endpoint or trust that client code won't be tampered with. This reality hits especially hard for deployments where customers call external APIs, public APIs, and open APIs from unsecured networks such as the Internet.

WARNING

Attackers regularly reverse-engineer client-side code or front-end code with tools that unpack, decompile, or disassemble application binaries. Attackers also make use of intercepting proxy tools such as Burp Suite or OWASP Zed Attack Proxy. These are the same proxying tools in use for general application troubleshooting and security assessment work. In the hands of a trained professional as well as an attacker, the tools are incredibly powerful. Be extra careful; always presume an endpoint is compromised along with the client-side code that runs on it. Back-end services (APIs) and the data they provide are the most valuable targets to attackers.

APIs underpin digital supply chains

Your organization's API ecosystem is more than just the APIs it builds. API integrations and API dependencies in acquired applications or online services round out any organization's portfolio. Collectively, all of these APIs form an expansive digital supply chain and increase the attack surface for organizations. The mixture of first-party and third-party APIs and infrastructure complicates what security controls are available to you, let alone what code may be visible.

WARNING

Attackers know this reality of distributed architectures and supplier integrations, and they often target the weakest link. In fact, attackers commonly exploit a weakness in an API as an initial attack vector and then pivot to other networks, servers, workloads, applications, and APIs. These multistep attack sequences often evade traditional security controls. The realities of API ecosystems further emphasize the need for runtime behavior analysis to detect novel exploits. Chapter 4 dives deeper into behavior analysis and runtime protection.

Taking a Closer Look at the OWASP API Security Top 10

The Open Web Application Security Project (OWASP) has grown in popularity over the years, and the Application Security Top 10 is frequently cited in the security industry. In 2019, OWASP published the API Security Top 10 to describe the ten most common API flaws. The list should be your starting point for understanding common weaknesses and vulnerabilities seen in APIs. Furthermore, this list is useful as a training and awareness aid, and it can also serves as a lightweight taxonomy for classifying issues seen in APIs.

REMEMBER

The sphere of concern over APIs shouldn't begin and end with the OWASP API Security Top 10. Attackers chain together exploits of flaws described in the OWASP API Security Top 10. They also employ automation to increase their chances of success and cause greater damage. For example, excessive data exposure and broken authentication leave an API susceptible to automated attacks such as enumeration and scraping. APIs designed in such a way are sometimes referred to as *leaky APIs*.

These sections discuss the OWASP API Security Top 10 sequentially because there's no easy way to group the flaws. Some entries like authentication, authorization, and injection flaws can seem redundant to the OWASP Application Security Top 10, but API context adds uniqueness. Other entries like improper assets management or insufficient logging and monitoring are fundamental to all systems engineering work. However, the problems become more pronounced with APIs because of rapid development cycles, undocumented API changes, and ongoing integration work.

API1:2019 Broken Object Level Authorization

Object level authorization is an access control mechanism used to validate an API caller's ability to access a given object. Even if an application implements proper authorization checks in infrastructure, developers often forget to apply these checks before allowing access.

Attackers easily exploit API endpoints that are vulnerable to *broken object level authorization (BOLA)* by manipulating the ID of an object that is sent within an API request. These vulnerabilities are extremely common in API-based applications because the server component often doesn't fully track the client's state. Instead, the server component relies on parameters like object IDs sent from the client to decide which objects can be accessed.

Every API endpoint that receives an ID of an object and performs any type of action on the object should implement object level authorization checks. These checks should be made continuously throughout a given session to validate that the authenticated user has access to perform the requested action on a requested object.

Failure to enforce authorization at the object level can lead to data exfiltration as well as unauthorized viewing, modification, or destruction of data. BOLA can also lead to full account takeover; for example, attackers can compromise a password reset flow and reset credentials of an account for which they aren't authorized.

API2:2019 Broken User Authentication

Authentication mechanisms are easy targets for attackers, particularly if the authentication mechanisms are fully exposed or public. Prompting users or machines for authentication material may also not be possible in some API use cases. These two points make the authentication component potentially vulnerable to many exploits.

Broken authentication in APIs originates from the following:

>> **Lack of protection mechanisms:** The API endpoint lacks an authentication mechanism. This is a common occurrence within internal networks or middleware.

>> **Improper or misconfigured authentication:** The mechanism is used or implemented without considering the attack vectors, or the mechanism isn't appropriate for the use case. For example, an authentication mechanism designed for IoT devices typically isn't the right choice for a web application like an ecommerce site.

This OWASP entry is a catch-all for all types of authentication issues including weak password complexity, inadequate account lockout thresholds, authentication material exposed in URLs, authentication tokens with insufficient entropy, use of API keys as the only authentication material, and lack of two-factor authentication (2FA).

WARNING

Attackers who are able to successfully exploit vulnerabilities in authentication mechanisms can take over user accounts, gain unauthorized access to data, make unauthorized transactions as other users, and abuse implicitly trusted connections to pivot attacks to other systems.

API3:2019 Excessive Data Exposure

Teams sometimes design applications such that back-end APIs provide all the data that might be necessary for a given function and then depend on client-side code to filter appropriately. Because APIs can be used as a means of data exchange for many types of API consumers, back-end engineers may implement APIs in a generic way without thinking about the sensitivity or privacy of data. Traditional security scanning and runtime detection tools can't differentiate between legitimate data returned from the API and sensitive data that shouldn't be returned. This level of analysis requires a deep understanding of the application design and API context.

Exploitation of excessive data exposure weaknesses is simple. Attackers sniff the API traffic generated by their interface, a client application running on a device such as a laptop or smartphone. They make use of the same intercepting proxy tools used by security practitioners to expose the network communications between the API client (the front-end code) and back-end APIs. After attackers expose traffic, they can analyze the API responses and look for data that is returned to the user but typically not displayed in the client interface.

API4:2019 Lack of Resources & Rate Limiting

API requests consume back-end resources such as network, CPU, memory, and storage. APIs don't always impose restrictions on the size or number of resources that can be requested by the client or user. Lack of rate and resource limiting doesn't just potentially impact performance of back-end compute though. Lack of limiting also opens the door to many types of attacks including Denial of Service (DoS), brute-forcing, enumeration, and credential stuffing.

Here is a closer look at how attackers exploit APIs that lack limits:

>> **Lack of resource limit:** Attackers exploit lack of resource limiting by crafting a single API call that can overwhelm an application, impacting the application's performance and responsiveness or causing it to become unresponsive. This type of attack is sometimes referred to as an *application-level DoS*. Lack of resource limits may leave the system, application, or API susceptible to authentication attacks and data exfiltration attacks.

>> **Lack of rate limit:** Attackers exploit the lack of rate limiting by crafting and submitting high volumes of API requests to overwhelm system resources, brute force login credentials, quickly enumerate through large data sets, or exfiltrate large amounts of data.

API5:2019 Broken Function Level Authorization

Broken function level authorization (BFLA) shares some similarity to BOLA, though the target with BFLA is API functions as opposed to objects that APIs interact with as in the case of BOLA. Attackers attempt to exploit both BOLA and BFLA when targeting APIs in order to escalate privileges horizontally or vertically.

Attackers discover BFLA flaws because API calls are structured and predictable. Finding vulnerable API endpoints is possible in the absence of API documentation or schema definitions by reverse engineering client-side code and intercepting application traffic. Some API endpoints might also be exposed to regular, nonprivileged users making BFLA flaws easier for attackers to discover.

Attackers exploit BFLA flaws by sending legitimate API requests to an API endpoint that they shouldn't have access to, or by intercepting and manipulating API requests originating from client applications. For example, attackers may change an HTTP method from GET to PUT. Alternatively, attackers may also alter a query parameter or message body variable such as changing the string "users" to "admins." Attackers exploit BFLA flaws to gain access to unauthorized resources, take over other accounts, modify accounts, or escalate privileges.

API6:2019 Mass Assignment

Modern application frameworks encourage developers to use functions that automatically bind input from the client into code variables and internal objects. The frameworks do this to help simplify and speed up development within the framework. Attackers can use this side effect of frameworks to their advantage by updating or overwriting properties of sensitive objects that developers never intended to expose. Mass assignment vulnerabilities are also sometimes referred to as *autobinding* or *object injection vulnerabilities*.

Exploitation of mass assignment vulnerabilities in APIs requires an understanding of the application's business logic, objects relations, and the API structure. APIs expose their underlying implementation along with property names by design. Attackers also gain further understanding by reverse engineering client-side code, reading API documentation, probing the API to guess object properties, exploring other API endpoints, or by providing additional object properties in request payloads to see how the API responds.

An API endpoint is vulnerable if it automatically converts client-provided data into internal object properties without considering the sensitivity and the exposure level of these properties. Binding client provided data like JSON attribute-values pairs to data models without proper filtering of properties based on an allowlist usually leads to mass assignment vulnerability.

Attackers exploiting mass assignment vulnerabilities can update object properties that they shouldn't have access to, allowing them to escalate privileges, tamper with data, and bypass security controls.

API7:2019 Security Misconfiguration

Security misconfigurations include insecure default configurations, incomplete configurations, open cloud storage, misconfigured HTTP headers, unnecessary HTTP methods, overly permissive cross-origin resource sharing (CORS) policies, and verbose error messages.

Attackers exploit security misconfigurations to gain knowledge of the application and API components during reconnaissance phases where attackers passively or stealthily gather information about a target or victim. Detailed errors such as stack trace errors can expose sensitive user data and system details that aid attackers during their reconnaissance phase to find exploitable technology including outdated or misconfigured web and application servers. Attackers also exploit misconfigurations to pivot their attacks, such as bypassing authentication due to misconfigured access control mechanisms.

Automated security scanners are available to detect common misconfigurations like unnecessary or legacy services. Where you detect these issues in a given technology stack varies greatly though. Vulnerability scanners may only scan a running server for known vulnerabilities and misconfigurations in published software, usually in the form of CVE IDs. However, this type of detection doesn't provide a complete picture because misconfigurations can exist in underlying code, in third-party dependencies, or other system integrations.

Organizations often employ a barrage of security scanners in build pipelines to try to catch as many issues as possible prior to production deployment. Cases where security misconfiguration is the result of something simple like a missing patch are often minimal. Most misconfigurations that lead to exploitable APIs are far stealthier and obscured by complex architectures.

API8:2019 Injection

Injection flaws are common in the web application space, and they also carry over to web APIs. Structured Query Language (SQL) injection, or SQLi, is one of the most well-known types of injection flaws. Other varieties of injection flaws impact a range of interpreters and parsers beyond just SQL including Lightweight Directory Access Protocol (LDAP), NoSQL, operating system (OS) commands, Extensible Markup Language (XML), and object-relational mapping (ORM).

Attackers exploit injection flaws by sending malicious data to an API that is in turn processed by an interpreter or parsed by the application server and passed to some integrated service, such as a database management system (DBMS) or a database as a service (DBaaS) in the case of SQLi. The interpreter or parser is essentially tricked into executing the unintended commands because they either lack the filtering directly or expect it to be filtered by other server-side code.

Successful exploitation of an injection flaw by attackers can lead to a wide range of impacts including information disclosure, data loss, and denial of service (DoS). In many cases, successful injection attacks expose large sets of unauthorized sensitive data. Attackers may also be able to create new functionality, perform remote code execution, or bypass authentication and authorization mechanisms altogether.

API9:2019 Improper Assets Management

Maintaining a complete, accurate API inventory is critical to understanding potential exposure and risk. An outdated or incomplete inventory results in unknown gaps in the API attack surface and makes identifying older versions of APIs that should be decommissioned more difficult. Similarly, inaccurate API documentation results in risks like unknown exposure of sensitive data and makes identifying vulnerabilities that need to be remediated difficult.

REMEMBER

Unknown APIs, referred to as *shadow APIs*, and forgotten APIs, referred to as *zombie APIs*, typically aren't monitored or protected by security tools. Known API endpoints may also have unknown or undocumented functionality, which are referred to as *shadow parameters*. As a result, these APIs and the infrastructures that serve them are often unpatched and vulnerable to attacks. Attackers may gain unauthorized access to sensitive data, or even gain full server access through old, unpatched, or vulnerable versions of APIs.

API10:2019 Insufficient Logging & Monitoring

Insufficient logging and monitoring of APIs enables attackers to perform reconnaissance, abuse business logic, compromise systems, maintain persistence, and move laterally across environments without being detected. The longer attackers dwell or are present in an environment, the higher the likelihood the attack will result in a breach, brand or reputation damage, or some other negative impact.

Without visibility over ongoing malicious activities, attackers have ample time to perform reconnaissance, pivot to other systems, and tamper with, extract or, destroy data.

Recognizing Automated Attack Patterns

Attackers frequently create or use custom code, python scripts, command line scripts, pre-built bots, and intercepting proxies to perpetuate and automate API attacks. New attack patterns emerge as attackers abuse the unique business logic that organizations build into their APIs. These sections cover two automated attack patterns that all industries face: credential stuffing and scraping.

Brute forcing, credential stuffing, and account takeover, oh my!

Brute force attacks are where attackers enumerate through alphanumeric sequences to find working username and password combinations that provide authenticated context. Brute force attacks often combine each username in a one (username)-to-many (password) attack. Attackers may also attempt to brute force usernames, depending on how much data they're starting with.

Credential stuffing relies on lists of compromised username/password combinations and the common bad habit of users implementing the same credentials across multiple services.

Where brute forcing and credential stuffing converge is the end goal of *account takeover (ATO)*. ATO is when attackers have obtained working credentials that provide them authenticated context in a system and its APIs. Once authenticated, attackers have access to sensitive data or functionality and may try to further escalate privileges.

STOPPING CREDENTIAL STUFFING ATTACKS

Finastra, a leading FinTech platform provider, frequently defends against credential stuffing attacks, with hackers automating account ID info in an effort to succeed at account takeover. The Finastra team has deployed API security from Salt Security to automatically detect and block these attacks, which otherwise easily pass through the company's WAFs and API gateways.

TIP

Credential stuffing and brute force attacks can be mitigated by implementing policies that lock an account after multiple login attempts. However, setting aggressive lockout thresholds can impact user experience. As a compromise, organizations sometimes implement a lax lockout policy, such as locking an account after ten consecutive, failed login attempts within an hour. The failed attempt counter resets after 60 minutes.

WARNING

However, attackers take advantage of these relaxed thresholds by backing off their login requests and pausing attempts until thresholds and counters reset. This attack technique is another example of why runtime behavior analysis is necessary to detect and prevent API abuse.

The plague of scraping

Public APIs carry inherent risk because the design leans toward allowing anonymous access, and traditional access control mechanisms are a luxury. It's not possible to enforce strong authentication and authorization without registering users or employing additional authentication factors such as 2FA. Such an approach can negatively impact user experience and service adoption.

Attackers take advantage of these exposed APIs with relaxed access controls. APIs may also expose too much data or lack rate limits, which are two common flaws described in the OWASP API Security Top 10 (refer to the section, "Taking a Closer Look at the OWASP API Security Top 10," earlier in this chapter). When these design flaws all apply to a given API endpoint, you end up with a leaky API that may inadvertently expose sensitive or private data. It's trivial for attackers to enumerate API endpoints and scrape data en masse using even basic scripts.

Attackers collect data at scale and in large volumes by utilizing the same data analytics tools that practitioners use to aggregate and correlate data to extract meaningful patterns. Depending on the information within the collected dataset, attackers may use scraped data to perpetuate fraud, social engineer individuals, target users with phishing attacks, or brute force accounts.

Chapter 4

Securing APIs

Traditional approaches can be beneficial to API observability and monitoring, and they also have usefulness for some aspects of security. However, a new approach is needed to protect APIs throughout their life cycles.

This chapter covers the importance of architecture in API security, and why a platform approach is needed to avoid the pitfalls of one-off tools and controls. I also describe the groupings of capabilities that are most critical for securing APIs throughout their life cycles: continuous discovery, protection, and remediation. This chapter also includes some API security best practices for all organizations to consider.

Recognizing Why Architecture Is Essential

The resulting gaps in API security posture that are left with traditional approaches has created the need for purpose-built API security. API security can't be addressed by a collection of splintered tools, stitched together by engineering teams, and operated haphazardly. This approach results in operational headaches, scaling issues, and increased likelihood of security incident. The following sections explain the importance of the architecture of any API security solution and core traits you should look for in a solution.

IN THEIR OWN WORDS

"Architecture is essential to effective API security. Only platforms with the ability to capture and analyze all your API traffic can create the context needed for full protection. You need a rich data engine and time-proven AI and ML algorithms to identify APIs and their exposed data, find and stop attackers, and distill the remediation details needed to harden vulnerable APIs."

— Curtis Simpson, CISO, Armis

Focusing on architecture

Any API security tooling you consider for your organization should be built as a platform of capabilities. API security strategy demands a full life cycle approach because security issues, vulnerabilities, logic flaws, and misconfigurations arise at different stages of API design, development, delivery, and operation.

REMEMBER

API security tooling should leverage Big Data to collect and store large amounts of API telemetry, correlate API traffic, provide context, and power fast attack detection and response. The tooling should also use AI/ML to continuously extract useful, actionable signals for IT teams. Time-in-market is another key consideration because algorithms improve over time through training and data sets are enriched by the network effect, with more users and API calls.

Identifying core traits in an API security platform

Any API security tooling you consider should be built with automation and cloud-scale capacity in mind. Realistically, that infers a cloud-native design, making use of cloud-born technologies such as auto-scaling infrastructure components, cloud storage, and cloud analytics. This approach enables support for all your organization's environments as API adoption increases.

Key architecture attributes that API security tooling should exhibit include the following:

>> **Environment agnostic:** API security tooling needs to support modern and legacy infrastructures regardless of where they're hosted. The tooling should also be able to integrate with network elements like load balancers, API gateways, and web application firewalls (WAFs).

>> **Independence from additional server agents and proxies:** API security tooling shouldn't require additional server agents or network proxies. The tooling should avoid the use of client-side code to stop attacks including CAPTCHAs or JavaScript in the traffic stream. These approaches create issues with front-end performance and are ineffective in direct API communication.

>> **Cloud-based storage and analytics:** API security tooling should make use of cloud-based storage and data analytics, often referred to as Big Data. This approach is the only way to retain enough data to inform baselines of API behaviors and consumption patterns, drive analysis engines, and identify potential data loss, privacy impact, or other security incident.

>> **AI/ML based analysis:** API security tooling should use AI/ML to analyze all the data and telemetry that are collected and produce meaningful security signals. Machine-assisted approaches are essential for powering detection and enforcement capabilities, such as determining where best to mitigate an API issue or what control is most appropriate. Machine-assisted analysis also helps reduce high false positive rates that are common in traditional approaches.

TIP

Ensure that API security tooling is designed to work in environments with encrypted transport. Some approaches suffer from reduced visibility with traffic inspection.

Evolving Your Catalog: A Continuous Discovery of APIs

Your API catalog will continuously evolve due to API development, API integration, and third-party API dependencies. DevOps practices also complicate matters with increased release velocity. You must continuously identify API endpoints and parameters, classify sensitive data they expose, and catalog your APIs to drive other API security activities.

WARNING

The API catalog that exists in your organization's API management platform, if it uses one, is likely incomplete. Configuration management and asset management databases are either too stale or too far removed from API context.

The following sections describe technological capabilities to seek for discovery and cataloging. And that discovery capability should also incorporate data classification to highlight what types of sensitive or private data are exposed.

Considering discovery capabilities you need

Due to the number of changes occurring normally in an organization and the pace of evolution, API discovery must be continuous. A point-in-time snapshot will be instantly stale the moment you can start coordinating activities or implementing controls. Here are the API discovery features you need:

>> **Span all environments and API types.** API security tooling should automatically collect data and metadata about APIs across environment types, including third-party API consumption. Discovery should be based on analysis of actual traffic and not just schema definitions to account for deviations between intended design and production deployments.

>> **Identify shadow APIs.** API security tooling should identify *shadow APIs,* which are unknown or undocumented APIs. This detection should include shadow API endpoints, API functions, and API parameters. These unknown API resources that have flown under the radar of operations and security teams result in additional attack vectors.

>> **Identify zombie APIs.** API security tooling should identify *zombie APIs,* which are outdated or deprecated APIs. Old versions and old code of APIs often linger when building or operating APIs at scale. Zombie endpoints can contain buggy or vulnerable code, may expose excessive data or functionality, may no longer be monitored, and may lack other production mitigations.

Many scanning tools focus on IP address and host information, which alone are insufficient for API security. Effective API discovery and cataloging must include all appropriate API metadata such as API endpoints and API functions, paths, and message body structures.

Incorporating data classification

APIs are used frequently to exchange data that may be sensitive. As a result, you want any API security tooling to identify any sensitive data types in API parameters and payloads as well as tag API endpoints appropriately so you're aware of potential exposures.

A range of personally identifiable information (PII) and other data types are subject to regulation. As examples, sensitive data includes protected health information (PHI) as defined by the Health Insurance Portability and Accountability Act (HIPAA), and private data includes information types defined by General Data Protection Regulation (GDPR).

Failing to identify and protect sensitive data can result in penalties from regulatory bodies, severe brand damage, or loss of customers. API discovery can be useful for audits and prioritizing API security activities.

Protecting APIs Continuously

Chapter 2 examines how mediating technologies like API gateways can provide elements of API runtime protection. Used alone though, these mediation mechanisms leave gaps in your API security posture. Traditional runtime security approaches either aren't designed for the world of APIs, or they fail to provide full API context. You need to seek API security capabilities that can detect API attacks early and provide protection that adjusts dynamically based on your changing API attack surface.

A common threat protection approach is to front-end API mediation points with additional proxies such as next-generation firewalls (NGFW) or WAFs. Such an approach adds latency and provides minimal to no added protection beyond the message inspection capabilities of most API gateways. Corresponding rules aren't designed for unique API business logic, and these mechanisms can't provide full context.

The following sections detail what detection and protection capabilities you should seek. Consider both sides of this coin as you select and implement any API protection.

Identifying the detection capabilities you need

You need capabilities that can identify API attacks quickly and early. WAFs and API gateways focus on transactions in isolation rather than viewing the whole picture of a complete API sequence to provide full context. API gateways, including those that exist as components of API management and integration platforms, are primarily API mediators and access control enforcers that may already be overloaded.

Schema-dependent API security tools fail at detecting certain types of API attacks, such as broken object level authorization (BOLA) flaws. Limitations are inherent when restricting security protection to API schema definitions at the expense of also examining traffic in runtime.

Some organizations may attempt to repurpose intrusion detection systems (IDS), intrusion prevention systems (IPS), and NGFW for API security, but these systems are even less suited for the task of API attack detection because they sacrifice any application layer or API focus for broad, multiprotocol attack detection. Detection capabilities you need include the following:

>> **Attacker correlation:** API security tooling should aggregate and correlate API traffic and associate it to attacker campaigns where applicable. Tooling should correlate attack behavior per source IP address, per user ID, and per session ID.

>> **Behavior analysis and anomaly detection:** API security tooling should programmatically parse API business logic and behaviors to assess impacts to an organization's API

security posture. Tooling should exhibit traits of user and entity behavior analytics (UEBA) to detect a wide range of API abuses and automated attacks where API consumption patterns deviate from baselines.

>> **Early attacker identification:** API security tooling should continuously detect API attacks early and quickly. Attackers go through an early reconnaissance phase as they passively and stealthily probe API targets. These passive analysis techniques evade most detections because they typically appear as legitimate traffic. API security tooling should detect subtle variations in API consumption patterns that result from automation scripts and reverse engineering tools employed by attackers.

Focusing on the protection capabilities you need

Expanding on API threat protection capabilities beyond what is afforded by traditional approaches is critical. Testing or detecting issues in APIs isn't enough. You need a more comprehensive approach if you desire to stop API attacks before attackers can exfiltrate data or do damage to your organization. Here are the protection capabilities you need:

>> **Stop attacks that exploit OWASP API Security Top 10 flaws.** API security tooling should stop attackers that attempt to exploit issues defined in the OWASP API Security Top 10 (refer to Chapter 3 for more about this list). The list includes exploits of BOLA flaws, BFLA flaws, broken authentication, excessive data exposure, lack of resource or rate limiting, security misconfigurations, and injection flaws.

>> **Block malicious requests while learning API logic.** API security tooling should block or mitigate API attacks while learning the organization's unique business logic. Some API attacks can be detected and stopped regardless of how an organization designs its APIs, including injection attacks and excessive API consumption.

>> **Stop credential stuffing and brute forcing attacks.** API security tooling should stop the automated attacks (see Chapter 3) where the end goal for an attacker is account takeover (ATO). ATO is a risk for any organization that

exposes an API where authentication and authorization are required. Even in cases where additional authentication factors are used, attackers combine techniques to overcome strong access controls.

>> **Stop application-layer denial of service (DoS) attacks.** API security tooling should stop application-layer DoS attacks. DoS and distributed DoS (DDoS) are often viewed from the lens of excessive traffic or request rates, or volumetric attacks. The more nefarious and stealthy form of DoS is application-layer DoS, or layer 7 DoS. Application-layer DoS is more difficult to stop because of application and API uniqueness. Ensure that the security tooling doesn't stop at layer 3 and 4 DoS. Tooling should also cover layer 7 DoS and for APIs specifically.

WARNING

Traditional rate limiting and message filtering mechanisms in API gateways or WAFs are too static, too operationally complex, or not well-maintained by the vendor. Use static limits if you have limited API consumption, but seek dynamic limiting mechanisms if your API consumers are numerous or traffic patterns are less predictable.

Remediating APIs: Enhancing Capabilities and Streamlining Workflow

DevOps and DevSecOps practices reinforce the notion of feedback loops. You want your tooling to be integrated and automated in such a way that workflow is seamless. Workflow is typically centered around git-based version control systems (VCS) and CI/CD pipelines. Security and nonsecurity teams should be able to quickly obtain the information they need to act on and resolve issues.

REMEMBER

Remediation workflow should be minimally disruptive to normal workstreams and business activity. In practice, you can achieve this by getting as much information and resolution capability into the toolchains that are used as part of normal work.

The following sections call out remediation capabilities you need and why adapting to response workflows is necessary.

Naming remediation capabilities you need

Organizations frequently wrestle with common vulnerabilities and exposures (CVE) IDs, often generated from vulnerability scanning. However, design flaws, software weaknesses, and business logic flaws don't map neatly to CVE IDs. With respect to API security, you need to seek remediation capabilities that can check for a wide spectrum of API-related flaws, vulnerabilities, and infrastructure misconfigurations. These remediation capabilities should work continuously for the full life cycle of APIs in development, build, and runtime phases.

REMEMBER

A security fix may not always be code level, because it may not be technically possible to fix a problem in code, it may not be feasible to produce a code fix in a timely manner, or it's more practical to mitigate through other infrastructure components. Here are API remediation capabilities you need:

>> **API vulnerability and weakness identification:** API security tooling should use a combination of techniques to assess the security of all APIs in the organization. Tooling should passively analyze API traffic that flows through numerous points of enterprise architecture on- and off-premises, and it should analyze API schema definitions when available to identify areas of API weakness that should be remediated by development teams, operations teams, or both.

>> **Remediation guidance tailored to personas:** API security tooling should provide remediation guidance focused on code-level fixes for development perspectives as well as infrastructure configurations for operations perspectives. Issues should be mapped to the OWASP API Security Top 10 (refer to Chapter 3) where appropriate, but technical details shouldn't be written only for security audiences.

>> **Integration with defect tracking systems:** API security tooling should integrate with external defect tracking systems to support pre-existing security and development workflows for remediation. Defect tracking may be handled in external DevOps suites, ITSM, or vulnerability management (VM) platforms depending on the organization's IT and security programs.

>> **Code repository and pipeline integration:** API security tooling should provide mechanisms to integrate with development, build, and release systems. Integration may be through VCS integration to statically analyze API code or schema definitions. Integration may also be through CI/CD integration to dynamically analyze APIs in runtime in preproduction or production environments.

Adapting your incident response processes for APIs

API attacks are inevitable, and your organization must deal with threat actors on multiple fronts. Even though API protection is key to defending your APIs in runtime, your organization's ability to respond in the event of an attack is just as critical. Not all API-related risks are attack-oriented either, where dominant concerns may include data exfiltration or scraping by an attacker. Your incident response playbooks should encompass many unforeseen API events including unintentional data exposure, privacy impacts, and availability issues.

REMEMBER

You need API-centric incident response capabilities that integrate with the work streams and tooling of development and SecOps teams. Data feeds into the organization's SIEM are a given, though it should be done intelligently to provide useful signals. Integration shouldn't be limited to a basic log feed or data dump. API security tooling should intelligently prioritize events, provide actionable security alerts, and support the work streams of a modern SOC and IT workforce.

Defining API Security Best Practices

The broad landscape of API design patterns and API consumer types complicates security requirements for your organization. The diversity of the API landscape makes arriving at a set of best practices challenging. Your security best practices must be comprehensive and inclusive of many technology areas.

APIs are implemented, operated, or interacted with by many roles within an organization including development, API product teams, API operations teams, application security teams, and security operations. As with DevOps practices, collaboration is crucial for building and operating secure APIs. The following sections detail a range of API security best practices you should consider adopting.

API discovery and cataloging

An accurate API inventory is critical to many aspects of IT within your organization. Compliance, risk, and privacy teams require API inventory, particularly as they must answer to regulatory bodies. Security teams also need API inventory so that they can have a realistic view of their attack surface and risk posture to help prioritize the wide range of API security activities that must be accounted for. Here are the discovery best practices:

» Discover APIs in lower environments and not just production. Lower environments often have lax security and make for primary attack targets.

» Include API dependencies and third-party APIs in your API catalog. Third-party APIs are part of the attack surface.

» Tag and label APIs and microservices as a DevOps best practice. Such processes also serve as enablers of many other API life cycle activities.

Security testing

Traditional scanning technologies struggle with parsing custom-developed code and business logic because design patterns and coding practices vary per developer. Use traditional security testing tools to verify certain elements of an API implementation such as well-known misconfigurations, vulnerabilities, and exploitable conditions, but you must operate these tools with awareness of the limitations. Testing best practices include the following:

» Statically analyze your API code for well-defined exploitable conditions in code as it's committed to VCS, built and delivered in CI/CD pipelines, or both.

» Check for known vulnerable third-party dependencies and open-source componentry in your API code.

» Dynamically analyze and fuzz deployed APIs to identify exploitable conditions in the fully integrated system.

API mediation and architecture

API mediation provides for improved visibility, accelerated delivery, increased operational flexibility, and improved enforcement capability. The latter is often used to enforce API access control. An organization can commonly achieve mediation by deploying API gateways and microgateways that function as reverse proxies, forward proxies, or both. The following are mediation best practices:

>> Mediate your APIs to improve observability and monitoring capabilities for inner and outer APIs.

>> Use mediation mechanisms like API gateways to enforce access control, rate limiting, and message filtering.

>> Augment your mediation mechanisms with API security tooling that can provide context and make the difference between static and dynamic control.

Network security

Traditional network perimeters erode as organizations move toward highly distributed APIs and cloud services. Infrastructure becomes more ephemeral, virtualized, and containerized. Consequently, this evolution makes some traditional network access control approaches ineffective. Modernized network security begins to heavily intersect with identity and access management (IAM), or "identity as the perimeter." The following are network security best practices:

>> Enable encrypted transport to protect the data your APIs transmit over unprotected networks.

>> Use IP address allow and deny lists if you have small numbers of API consumers, such as with partner or supplier integration use cases.

>> Look to dynamic rate limiting for API deployments where API consumers are too numerous or too unpredictable.

Data security

Appropriate techniques for securing data include masking, tokenizing, or encrypting. Many data security efforts focus on securing data at rest in a back-end system, such as database encryption or field-level encryption. These encryption approaches don't protect your data in cases where attackers obtain a credential or authorized session because the data will be decrypted for them when accessed through an API. Data security best practices include the following:

>> Use encryption selectively and as mandated by regulation due to operational complexity. Transport protection suffices for most API use cases.

>> Avoid sending too much data to API callers and relying on the API client or front-end to filter data. Sensitive or private data is always visible in traffic.

>> Adjust for modern threats like scraping or data inference where encryption isn't an effective mitigation.

Authentication and authorization

Authentication (authN) and authorization (authZ), and by extension identity and access management (IAM), are foundational to all security domains, including API security. IAM is used heavily for access control to functionality and data. When implementing authN and authZ, you must account for user identities as well as machine identities. Even though it's possible to challenge a user for additional authentication material in a session, this option isn't available for machine communication. AuthN and authZ best practices include the following:

>> Continuously authenticate and authorize API consumers throughout a session and based on behaviors, not just initially during login.

>> Use modern authN and authZ protocols like OpenID Connect (OIDC) and OAuth2.

>> Avoid using API keys as a sole means of authentication. API keys are primarily version control and should be paired with other authentication.

Runtime protection

Runtime protection, sometimes referred to as *threat protection*, is often delivered through proxies like API gateways and WAFs.

These mechanisms rely on message filters and static signatures, which can catch some types of attacks that follow well-defined patterns but miss most forms of API abuse. Runtime protections are useful for identifying misconfigurations in API infrastructure as well as behavior anomalies like credential stuffing, brute forcing, or scraping attempts by attackers. Runtime protection best practices include the following:

» Enable threat protection features within your API gateways and API management to mitigate risk of injection flaws like JSON and XML injection.

» Ensure that DoS and DDoS mitigation are part of your API protection approach. If attackers can't exploit or abuse an API, they often revert to DoS techniques.

» Augment traditional runtime controls with AI/ML and behavior analysis engines to detect novel API attacks where pre-built signatures leave gaps.

Chapter 5

Ten Things You Can Do Now to Secure APIs

Not sure about what you can do to secure APIs in your organization? What follows is a list of ten high-priority items you should focus on to identify and protect your APIs:

» **Identify API security leads.** Start with your application security team if you have one and identify API security leads to collaborate on discovery, testing, protection, and incident response. Your API security expertise may be scattered across development, infrastructure, operations, and security roles. Or you may find that expertise is concentrated within API product teams.

» **Deploy API-specific runtime protection.** Attackers regularly aim to exploit or abuse APIs. Data exposures and privacy impacts can be just as damaging if not more. Seek protections that can analyze API behaviors real time to detect and stop attackers early.

» **Adapt incident response for APIs.** Augment your digital forensics and incident response processes for the world of APIs. API abuse and data exposures may not rank high on the list initially, but successful API attacks have massive impact for organizations. Ensure that SecOps teams have what they need so they can respond quickly and loop in appropriate API expertise.

» **Define API remediation process.** As you discover, test, and protect APIs, you'll inevitably find code-level flaws or misconfigurations that leave APIs vulnerable. Formalize your remediation steps that also help power feedback loops critical in DevOps. Remediation often requires a mix of roles and can also include third parties.

» **Establish an API inventory.** Build an initial API inventory and plan to maintain it as your API landscape evolves. Your API inventory is more than what is contained in asset management databases or API management. You'll need discovery mechanisms that can identify API endpoints, gather metadata, and classify potentially exposed data types.

» **Identify shadow and zombie APIs.** API inventory and API schema definitions will only carry you so far. You'll need to scan on-premises and cloud environments continuously for *shadow* (undocumented) and *zombie* (outdated) APIs. These APIs present a significant security risk and are quickly uncovered by attackers.

» **Classify data types in APIs.** API discovery is useful for prioritizing where to place security controls or where to monitor more heavily, and for identifying and classifying potential data exposures. Data may be classified as sensitive or private depending on regulation. This form of API-specific data classification is critical for governance, risk, compliance, and privacy initiatives.

» **Analyze API schema and code.** Scanning for flaws early and prior to production delivery is promoted as part of security best practice. Such an approach can save IT cycles and reduce the likelihood that an attacker will find exploitable conditions. Continuously analyze API schema, scan code during build phases, and/or scan deployed APIs in runtime for exploitable conditions.

» **Skill up on modern architecture.** Understanding distinctions between monolith and microservices, inner and outer APIs, and cloud-native design patterns is useful for determining where best to discover, mediate, and protect APIs. Your security approach can't rely on controlling a network perimeter, because in modern architectures the perimeter has eroded.

» **Work toward a holistic API security strategy.** Expand your application security program (if you have one) to include network and infrastructure elements. Establish a regular cadence with security and development teams to review API roadmaps, best practices, and issues. Document, iterate, and improve over time.